TOLEDO:
... ITS ART
... AND ITS HISTORY.

(AN ILLUSTRATED ARTISTIC GUIDE)

Text:
RUFINO MIRANDA

English translation:
MARGARET McCLAFFERTY and
DAVID FRICKER

© EXCLUSIVE DIST.: JULIO DE LA CRUZ
CIUDAD, 3
45002 TOLEDO
Tel.: 925 22 28 09
Fax: 925 25 26 79

Printed by: Ediciones Savir S.A.
I.S.B.N.: 84-87318-01-0
D.L. TO: 1285-2000
Photography: **Fernando Garrido** - Oronoz - Foima - Manipel - José Ramón
The historical photographs of the City were kindly supplied by Toledo Town Hall.

Introduction

Two thousand years have passed since the name of Toledo entered recorded history. The Roman historian, Titus Livius, mentioned Toledo in his descriptions of the doings of Marcus Fulvius, who conquered the city at the head of the Roman legions. He wrote: "Toletum, ibi parva urbis erat, set loco munito".

Much has been written about the city since then. In the attempt to decipher the palimpsest of the civilizations which have left their mark on the city, poets, archaeologists, philosophers, historians and even theologians have investigated its every aspect, casting light on its most secret places and describing its monuments.

For centuries, wise men and artists have tried to solve the enigma of this multi-cultural city. It has been the meeting place for many different races, a melting pot of ideas and the birthplace of original culture. However, like all places with a special destiny, Toledo jealously guards one final secret, one not written in any book, and which is only revealed by personal experience.

To enjoy the experience of Toledo is not comparable to turning the pages of a history book, as the city is not a mere chapter in the history of Spain: it is the expression of Spanish history itself.

This book is neither a work of investigation, nor does it set out new theories or hypotheses to explain matters already studied and verified.

Some books written on the subject of Toledo have already become classics. However, they are useful only as works of reference, hard to come across and difficult to read. Others are specialized monographs, long, detailed and useless for the rushed modern tourist. On the other hand, there are the books designed for sale as souvenirs, which are full of colourful pictures and contain little information.

The author tries to fill the gap between these two extremes with this book. In the first instance, he wishes to complete and modernize all investigations carried out to date and, as the aim of this guide is to cover all that can be seen in one long day's visit, he has limited himself to what is accessible in that period of time. He has also taken care to portray the historical context of each of the monuments he describes, in order to make its creation and the reason for its existence more understandable.

This book is like a ray of light, an aid to the traveller, and later is of help in refreshing his memory.

One must go through the conventual quarter, set apart from mundane bustle in the silvery silence of the night, whispering so as not to break the silence, which is broken only by the monastic bell. At dawn, from the other side of the river valley, one must contemplate how the sun gilds the polychromatic ochre shades of the bricks, or the grey granite of the large porches. One must lose oneself in the ruggedness of the streets when, at sunset, the city slackens its pace, and the powers of magic flow forth.

Deciphering Toledo is an intimate and personal experience.

RUFINO MIRANDA,

TOLEDO

its Art and

its History

Panoramic view

New Bisagra Gate

Emperor Charles V decided to improve the appearance of the city by enlarging and remodelling the Alcázar palace, while at the same time giving the city a suitable main gate.

The gullies and rough patches on the road to Madrid had already been smoothed out when Parliament was held in Toledo in 1538. Nicolás de Vergara the older was given the job of renovating the old medieval city gate. While he respected the bases of the twin towers, he remodelled the room used by the gate keeper.

The architect Alonso de Covarrubias later went on to extend the space within the gate to create an extensive courtyard. He also designed the facade which can be seen nowadays, and added the semicircular towers on each side of the central Gateway. These are in dressed stone, on which a fine imperial shield in granite stands out, surmounted by a double - headed eagle.

Although the commemorative stone plaque here states that work on the gate finished in 1550, at a time when four generations of the royal family were alive (Juana "the mad", Charles the emperor, his son the future Philip II and the unfortunate prince Carlos), it is known that final works were undertaken around 1575. It was then that Nicolás de Vergara the younger added a second level onto the Arab towers, completing them with spires of glazed tiles. He also sculpted the image of Saint Eugenio.

The Bisagra Gate lies on the natural route into the city, at what has always been its most accessible point. This is where it gives onto the northern plain, called the **"Saqra"** by the Arabs because of the reddish colour of its soil. Thus in spite of the numerous controversies which have taken place over the years as to the origins of this gate's name, it is **"Bab - Sagra"**, i.e., the Sagra Gate.

In 1968, a piece of stone with an incomplete cufic inscription was found. It contains the name of Imael Al - Zafir (1032 - 1044) who founded the Toledan Taifa. He was father of the famous Al -Mamún. If this stone is related to the construction of the original gate, then it must date from the first half of the XI century.

As the two gates are hardly 80 metres apart, there is controversy as to which of them is the original Bisagra. The gate described above is generally known as the Puerta Nueva (New Gate), while the old gate has been renamed the **Puerta de Alfonso VI**, as it is thought that he passed under it when Christian troops entered the city on its reconquest, on May 25th, 1085.

The Old Bisagra Gate or Alfonso VI Gate

This is certainly the city gate which has suffered fewest alterations, and still has an almost completely original facade. This is due to its being covered for many years after the new gate was opened during the times of Charles V.

The originality of this gate, in a well defended angle of the walls with two additional flanking towers, next to the "Macbora" (cemetery) means that it must have once been the main gate of the city, and could hardly have been a side or less important gate.

The proportions and stone work of its horse shoe arch date it as being X century. A floral carving on the key stone of the arch dates from Visigoth times. The strangest feature of this gate is the enormous granite lintel, the presence of which has never been satisfactorily explained.

A blocked up side gate can be seen in the tower on the right, while the upper parts are XIII century Mudejar work, as can be seen from the bricks and style of the building work.

Alfonso VI Gate

In 1905 the gate was cleaned, and the side nearest the city demolished to create an attractive courtyard. It is to be hoped that considerations of taste and respect will eventually bring about the removal of a modern "sculpture" placed here.

10 *Bisagra Gate*

The Puerta del Sol (Sun Gate)

The steep hill up into the city through the **Bab-al-Mardum** (Gate of Cristo de la Luz) is impassibe for wagons and tiring for horses. It was therefore necessary to lay out another easier route following the line of the city wall. The entrance to this new way up into the city is through the **Puerta del Sol**.

In spite of its position outside and perpendicular to the wall, it is nonetheless a true entrance into the city.

It was built during the times of Archbishop Tenorio (1375 - 1399). It is thought to be the finest Mudejar style gate in Spain, combining strength and harmonious lines.

The round towers are built in rubble work, and the matching pointed and horseshoe shaped arches in are granite. The decorative work of the two sets of arches, the parapets and battlements, and the inside of the gate are in brick. This combination of building materials is very common in Mudejar work.

A medallion containing a triangle showing the ordination of Saint Idelfonso was placed above the horseshoe arch in the XVI century. Many years later a sun and moon were painted on either side of the medallion, and thus about two hundred years ago the gate ceased being known as the "Gate of the Blacksmith's", being renamed "The Puerta del Sol" ("Gate of the Sun").

Detail of the sixteenth century medallion

There is a small window in the first frieze of interlocking arches. This was used for carrier pigeons. Under this window is a marble embossing taken from a paleochristian sarcophagus. It shows the denial of Saint Peter.

The Gate of the Sun

13

The Cambrón Gate

The **Cambrón Gate** stands In the walls that run from the Old Bisagra Gate to San Martin Bridge. It is located at the place where a very large water course runs out of the city during rains, and must therefore date from the earliest times.

It has been identified as the **Bab al - Yahud**, or Gate of the Jews. This city gate is often mentioned in documents from the XII century onwards, and gave entrance to the populous Jewish quarter of the city.

Part of the original structure is still conserved in the outer part of the gate, in the form of the opening with a square tower at either side. In the base of these towers can be seen two large Arab memorial stones, taken from the nearby cemetery. On one of these stones the original inscription can still be seen.

The gate suffered a complete transformation during general reforms undertaken during the second half of the XVI century. Work on the gate was directed by Nicolas de Vergara the younger.

Two new towers were added to the gate, making it symmetrical and creating a small internal courtyard. The first floor of the gate house was renovated so that it could be used as living quarters for the gate keeper and guards. The facade was changed, and the shield of the Royal family added. A beautiful sculpture by Berruguete of Saint Leocardia, martyr and patron of the city, was placed inside the gate.

The Gate still has its old iron - covered doors. In 1577 the Queen granted the city the special privilege of not having to shut these every night.

The name "Cambrón" (hawthorn) first appeared during the middle of the XV century. The origins of this name are obscure, although it could come from the hawthorn trees which used to grow in abundance around the gate, while one of them even took root in one of the towers.

Not far from the gate a rectangular tower stands out over the wall. Among the granite stones of which it is built, others of limestone can be seen, these latter being of Visigoth origin. This is known as the *Torre de los Abades (Abotts' Tower)* as it was valiantly defended by Archbishop Don Bernardo and his canons during the Almoravid invasions, which took place between 1090 and 1099.

Cambrón Gate

15

St. John of the Kings

Saint John of the Kings

This fine church ("San Juan de los Reyes") lies just a bowshot from the Cambrón Gate. It is built on an area of relatively flat land in the Jewish quarter. From the viewing platform just in front of the church there is a view of the hills and houses ("Cigarralles") on the other side of the river and the plain of the Vega. The church is surmounted by an octagonal dome and flanked by buttresses.

The origins of this church go back to the *Battle of Toro*, in 1476, between followers of the Beltraneja family and those faithful to the young princess Isabel and prince Ferdinand. This battle decided the succession of the Throne of Castile.

Victory in the battle went to the Royal couple, and to crown the occasion Isabel decided to build a monastery as a votive temple and Royal pantheon.

The **architect** - sculptor was Hans Waas (a name rendered Juan Guas in Spanish). He was born in a village in Brittany, Saint - Paul de León, and came to Toledo while still a child with his father, Pedro. They came as Pedro was a member of the group of sculptors who travelled with Hanequin of Brussels. The boy was brought up and educated in Toledo, where he eventually married a girl from Torrijos, Marina Alverez. His education as a sculptor culminated in his work on the Door of the Lions of the Cathedral, working with the group of Flemish sculptors entrusted with the work.

He worked in a luminous style, although his roots and artistic vocabulary were founded in Toledo. San Juan de los Reyes is therefore in a gothic style, although it draws inspiration from the core of the local Mudejar style.

The church: This has a single aisle composed of four sections of extremely complex vaulting. There is a **Royal Gallery** above the columns which give access to the transept. The stonework here is better described in terms of fine jewellery than those of stone masonry.

Around the Royal Gallery run the initials of the royal names, F and Y, finishing in a fretwork parapet.

The walls of **the Presbytery** which was to have housed the royal tombs are decorated in the most lavish style. Never has the rhythmic repetition of a heraldic design given rise to a decorative effect of such beauty.

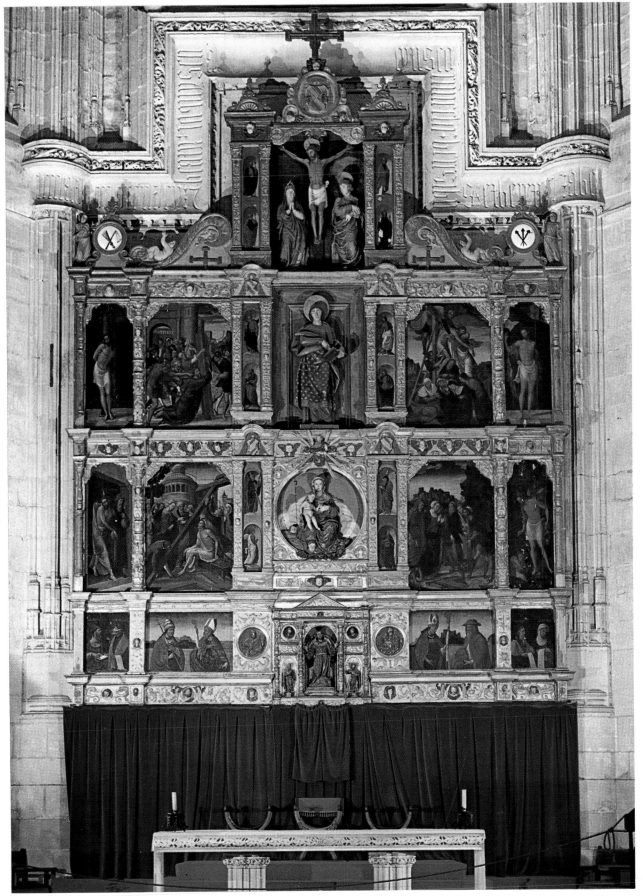

St. John of the Kings: reredos

The church is dedicated to Saint John, and his eagle holds the royal shields in its talons. These are flanked by the yoke and arrows.

There may be other, purer examples of the gothic, but none that is richer or more amazing.

The screen behind the altar. The original, together with the stalls and library, was destroyed during the sacking which the church suffered during the Napoleonic wars. The one now in place is by Francisco de Comontes, and was brought here from the Santa Cruz Hospital. Its origins are shown by the shields of the Mendoza family which it contains.

Above the screen behind the altar is a beautiful painting showing "The Allegory of the Defense of the Dogma of the Conception", painted by Romero Carrión, an artist who died young, in 1967.

Lower cloisters

The cloisters. When Juan Guas died in 1496, his co-workers, the Egas brothers, carried on with the construction of the cloisters, which were finished in 1504.

The harmony of proportion to be found in its broad windows is emphasized by the extremely fine mullions, and is enhanced by the fretwork decoration, which attains the delicacy of lace. A set of statues lines the four galleries.

The windows of the **upper cloister** are in a mixed (curved - straight - curved) style. They are the personal creation of Guas, while the roof is multi-coloured woodwork and was a later addition. The yoke and arrows and the emblems of the different kingdoms of Spain are rhythmically repeated.

The door in the **outside wall** of the cloisters was added at a much later date. It follows a design by Covarrubias (1610) and is not worthy of the building as a whole.

The chains and manacles of Christians once held prisoner hang from the granite walls. These prisoners were released during the gradual conquest of the forts and castles of the Nazarí kingdom, a process which culminated in the surrender of Granada on the 2-I-1492.

Lower cloisters

CLOISTERS

Panelling

The Upper cloisters

Santa Maria la Blanca Synagogue

Of the ancient splendour of the Toledo Synagogues, the richest and most prestigious of all those within the **Sepharad**, only two still stand. The memory of another lives on in a street name.

Many theories have grown around the beautiful and original synagogue now known as Santa Maria la Blanca ("Saint Mary the White"). These theories are attempts to date the building, as well as explaining its liturgical purpose and artistic style.

Some believe that this is the building constructed by Jusef ben Jossan (d. 1205) the tax collector of Alfonso VIII. Others state that it is the synagogue known as "Al Malikin" or Abu - DARHAM, and date it from the end of the XIII century, its construction having been paid for by David ben Solomón ben Abi - Durham (d. 1270).

The system of illumination used in this building in antiquity has never been satisfactorily explained: the bulls - eye windows which can be seen nowadays are a relatively recent addition. One theory is that originally the roofs of the aisles sloped down on each side from their centres, thereby allowing light to enter inside the building through what are now blind windows.

The **main facade** was the East wall, in which the small blocked up entrance door may be seen.

Nor is there any certainty as to where the ladies' gallery was located. One theory is that the building used to be longer, reaching into what is now the garden. This would explain the beams incorporated in the base of what is now the main door, as they could have been the supports for the timber framework of the gallery floor. However, excavations carried out in 1987 - 88 did not find any foundations.

The **inside** of the building is laid out as a small church, some 28 metres long by 20 wide. It is divided into five aisles, with octagonal pillars supporting beautiful horse-shoe arches. These pillars are crowned by fine stucco capitals, the only ones of their kind.

The history of this building can be divided into three distinct phases:

Phase one covers its construction during the middle years of the XIII century. Its irregular ground plan is only explicable by its having used the foundations of an earlier building. Only the south wall follows asymetrical axis. For the first time in Toledo octagonal brick pillars were used, instead of the columns usually taken from some demolished building.

During the second phase, an ingenious artist influenced by the style of Granada decorated the aisles, embellished the pillars with capitals and added the medallions with their complex geometrical knotted designs. The third phase saw the changes made during the times of Cardinal Siliceo during the mid XVI century. Then the wall where the rolls had been kept was transformed into the high altar, the doorway currently in use was added, and at the head of the building the scalloped domes were added for two new altars.

The edges of the friezes around the nave were sure to have been covered in inscriptions erased, as was the polychrome work, when the building was reconsecrated as a church.

Although **the capitals** are plasterwork, they are decorated by sculpting with a gouge rather than moulded. This can be seen from the fact that even though the same themes are repeated on different capitals, slight differences can be found between them.

The medallions above the columns show a richness of outstandingly beautiful intricate geometrical designs.

The synagogue was reconsecrated for Christian worship around the year 1405. Like many other singular buildings, it has been used for a wide variety of purposes, including those of church worship, barracks and as a warehouse.

The miracle is that it has survived so many troubles down to the present day.

The Synagogue of Samuel Levy (also known as the Transito)

Once the expulsion of the Jews had taken place, the beautiful synagogue of R. Samuel Ha-Levy passed into Christian hands. Here, the inscriptions were fortunately respected, and today are not only the finest group to survive from the whole middle ages, but also supply invaluable data for placing the building in its correct historical context.

The main painting in the retable while the building was being used as a church was by Correa de Vivar. As it showed the Assumption or Transit of the Virgin, the building came to be known by the hybrid name of the "Synagoga del Transito".

The inscriptions tell us that the synagogue was inaugurated during the month of TISRI, at the close of the Seder holidays in the year of the Jewish calendar 5,117, i.e., in 1357 AD.

Two inscriptions on the outer walls were still legible during the XVIII century. One said: *"This is the door of Jehovah, through which the just enter"*. The other was higher, next to the bell-cote, and read: *"Open the doors, that a just people may enter, guardians of loyalty"*.

As is usual, nothing about the outside of the building gives any sign of the ornamental richness awaiting inside. The large nave is 23 metres long by 9.5 wide, and is covered by a hand-carved ceiling of larch wood, one of the finest in Spain.

28

The east wall is sumptuously decorated. In the centre of this wall there is a niche *(Hekal)* where an ark or cupboard *(Arón)* could be placed to keep the Sacred Rolls *(Sepharim)* containing the Law *(Torah)*. On either side of this niche there are inscriptions praising R. Samuel Ha-Levy - "A man raised to the highest, may his God go with him and extol him! He has found grace and mercy under the wings of the mighty great-winged eagle, warrior valiant above all others, the great Monarch our lord and master, our King Don Pedro".

In the floor in front of the Hekal there is a remnant of the old floor of glazed tiles.

The Toledan craftsmen decorated all four walls with two bands, one above the other. The upper band combines blind windows with others open to the light, which was filtered by beautiful lattices. The lower band has the shields of Castile and León, intertwining with a border of Arabic lettering and floral themes. This is one of the most innovative examples of Toledan Gothic - Mudejar style, which although it has a clearly Christian inspiration, is realistic beyond the limitations of a purely Gothic style, expressing an Oriental accent and rhythm.

All of these details are framed by the Psalms of David, which are inscribed in beautifully executed Hebrew characters parallel to the decorative bands around the walls.

In the south wall there are large windows which open onto the Ladies' gallery. The decoration of this was very much deteriorated, although it was restored in 1988, and now rivals that of the Oratory.

The Sephardic Museum

This is located in rooms next to the nave of the synagogue. The few remaining testimonials of Hebrew culture in Toledo have been brought together here, together with others from all over Spain.

The large granite tombstones are of outstanding archeological value. Several correspond to victims of the black plague in 1348 - 9, who were buried in the old cemetery of Toledo.

The carved beam dated 1180 is perhaps the oldest remnant of a long vanished synagogue.

There is a capital inscribed in Hebrew and Arabic, which says: "blessed be you on your entrance and on your leaving".

The bowl from Tarragona is in scribed in three different languages, and dates from the VI century. It is decorated with Hebrew and Christian symbols.

The display cabinets contain utensils and objects used in rituals associated with different holy days. A magnificent roll of the TORAH stands out, together with lamps used during the Hanukkah, trays and cups of the Pesah and bridal robes from the Sephardies of the Magreb.

The House and Museum of El Greco

It is known from documents that El Greco lived in the abandoned palace belonging to the Marquis de Villena. Duke of Escalona, which stood on the site of what is now the Transito Park and its adjacent houses.

The building now fancifully known as the House of El Greco was in fact the palace of Samuel Levi, King Don Pedro's treasurer. It later passed into the hands of the "old" Duchess, Doña Aldonza de Mendoza, Duchess of Arjona.

SOROLLA: portrait of the Marquis de la Vega-Inclán

During the early years of the 20th century the Marquis de la Vega - Inclan converted the old palace into a museum to hold El Greco's paintings. In doing this he created a replica of what the painter's mansion could have been like, using furniture from the time of El Greco to create a suitable atmosphere.

There is an attractive **patio** with a tiled baseboard. From here, the dining room and a small sewing room for Doña Jerónima can be entered. She was the painter's companion and mother of his child, Jose Manuel.

The picturesque **kitchen** gives onto the large garden, under which are the vaults where Samuel Levi kept his treasure.

The dining room

A doorway surrounded by plasterwork is the entrance to the dining room. In the centre of the lintel there is a cross flanked by shields.

There are two steps up to the dining room. Its atmosphere and furnishings are normal, with tables, chairs and cupboards of all types.

The monks armchairs are of embossed leather, in the 16th century style. The outstanding item of furniture in this room is the wardrobe, with its drawers and marquetry work.

The living room

This is the other room on the ground floor that may be entered from the patio, although it only has one step. It is divided into three areas: the central area, with a wooden floor, is given atmosphere by a dark XVI century mirror, a table, monks' armchairs covered in velvet and silk, and a small lattice window overlooking the patio. The side area has a large trellised balcony, screened with a latticed window that overlooks the garden. This balcony is like a small drawing room or sewing room, and has an intimate and secluded atmosphere. The furniture here is smaller, and there is also a water colour of the Virgin and Child in the Italian - Flemish style of the XV/XVI century. There is also a portrait of Felipe II by a painter close to the circle of Sanchez Coello.

The kitchen

This room completes the ground floor. It too has a door opening onto the patio, like the other rooms overlooking the porch, above the high garden. It is in the style of a working kitchen, with a hearth and fireplace. There are continuous benches around the walls, and low everyday three - legged chairs. All of the kitchen utensils are close to the heating rings of the fire and the hearth, together with other everyday household objects. There are irons for the fire, and pots and oil lamps. The room is completed by a nice collection of ceramic ware, and is furnished with wardrobes, cupboards, low tables and chairs. The cupboards built into the walls are especially charming, and one has a relief depiction of the cross on its doors. This may make one think that they originally came from a convent. The other cupboard has fretwork on its doors, allowing its contents to be seen. Although the plates and jugs inside cannot be seen clearly, they certainly lend the cupboard charm by allowing a glimpse, but only a glimpse, of what is inside.

Bowl from Puente de Arzobispo

Among the ceramic items, a pair of bowls decorated with the typical motif of Talavera really stand out. They are decorated by oriental style winged animals, with hares and birds. These are set in a wooded landscape, allowing the artist to experiment with greens and yellows, bordered by manganese black. It must be taken into consideration that the clays and pottery ware of the Talavera and Puente del Arzobispo became mingled and intermixed in the XVII century. These pieces may well date from this period of change.

Another outstanding item is a large round serving dish. It has corrugated edges and a round - handled lid. This graceful piece is typical of the XVII Talavera style. It is in the Baroque style, in which the blues and whites are well contrasted, and the shine of the enamelwork makes it especially appealing. It is an example of the tendency, common in Talavera at that time, towards oriental themes in decoration. The lid may not belong to the piece.

Serving dish with lid (17th century)

Detail of the patio

Detail of the patio

The house of El Greco (patio)

The studio is on the **upper floor**. This contains an extraordinary version of the "Tears of Saint Peter", together with several everyday objects, just as if they were ready for El Greco to use.

One picture stands out from those which are merely exhibited to make up numbers. This is the "View and Plan of Toledo", dating from El Greco's last period (1604 - 1614). The virgin is descending surrounded by angels over a strange Toledan country estate. A boy holds a map which is minutely detailed and annotated. This document is essential for understanding the theories of El Greco, due to which he altered the actual positions of buildings in his pictures.

There are also paintings of all the apostles, together with a few sketches. In a downstairs room there is the hallucinatory picture of Saint Bernadino. Here El Greco elongated the body of the saint in an attempt to express spirituality. The mitres symbolize the three bishoprics which the saint renounced: Sienna, Ferrara and Urbino.

38   *The entrance hall of the house*

The ornamental cloth of
the Virgin with Child
(15th-16th Century)

Portrait of Felipe II
(school of Sánchez Coello)

Hispano-Flemish canvas
(15th century)

Stairs to the Upper Gallery

The study

The Tears of
St. Peter

The bedroom

Antechamber of the drawing room

Altarpiece of St. Bernard

View and plan of Toledo (El Greco)

The Cathedral History

The power of the Almohad factions of the Arabs in Spain was definitively restricted by the Battle of Navas de Tolosa (1212) known as "the Unfortunate" in Arab chronicles.

Toledo was no longer a frontier city, ceasing to be vulnerable to Arab attack.

Alfonso VIII and his councillor and aid Archbishop Ximénez de Rada did consider building a cathedral to commemorate the victory. The archbishop was "a learned and eminent man", who spoke several languages and had studied at the Universities of Paris and Bologna. However, the king died two years later.

Although in Leon and Burgos the cathedrals were being readied for their roofs, the Primal See in Toledo was still using the old mosque, which had been reconsecrated as the Main Church in 1086 by Alfonso VI. However, work here was started in 1221. In 1222 Pope Honorio III devoted a Bull to obtaining resources "as such a great work cannot be finished without great expense...". The first stone was ceremoniously laid in 1226, when work was already well under way.

Virtually nothing is known of the architect of the cathedral. Documents do mention a **Master Builder Martin** in 1227, and there is also a famous tombstone which reads: "**Petras Petri** magister eclesia... qui preseus templus construxit". It is not known where either of these men came from.

Even if **Master Martin** was not French, it is clear that he must have had in - depth knowledge of the plans and techniques used in French cathedrals, especially that at Le Mans. This is the case even though in Toledo the methods used are of unprecedented originality, especially in the ambulatory and flying buttresses at the head of the church.

The triforium gallery shows marked Toledo Mudejar influence, which may mean that it was built by **Pedro Pérez** (Petrus Petri) who continued the work of Master Martin. It is clearly of local inspiration, the work of an architect from the area of Toledo.

The West Front

As in other Gothic cathedrals, it was planned to give the main facade two symmetrical towers. However, in Toledo only the bell - tower was completed. It is 92 metres high, and contains the bell known as the "Gorda" ('The Big One'), which weighs almost 18,000 kilograms. The tower is surmounted by a strange conical "cruet". This is wooden - framed and is covered in slate, and has three spiked crowns.

The other tower terminates in a lower octagonal dome. This was built by Jorge Manuel, the son of El Greco.

The towers are on either side of the facade with its three doors.

The **Pardon Door** is in the centre. It gets its name from the indulgences which were granted to those who passed through this door. The **Judgement Door** on the right is so named due to the subject shown on its tympanum, although it is also known as the Door of the Notaries. The **left - hand door** is known as both the Hell Door and the Palm Door.

The west front was restored so thoroughly in the XVIII century using granite that it lost much of its original character.

Only the three doors were left as they were. The tympanum of the central door shows the Elevation. In the central column, Christ appears in his majesty presiding over the assembled apostles: although documents mention that this was begun in 1418, both style and craftwork correspond to the time of the doors themselves, which are dated 1337.

The Chapinería (or Clock) Door

This door corresponds to the North transept, and lies between the walls of the chapels of St. Peter and the Virgin of the Ciborium (Sagrario), forming a porch. It is protected by a splendid grille, shaped by Master Paulo in the time of Cardinal Mendoza (the end of the XV century).

This is without doubt the oldest door, and it is also the most interesting and mysterious, due to the difficulty of interpreting the passages carved around the tympanum, and the decoration of the jambs and lintel, and the relief work in the small vault.

It is a pity that during the XVIII century a new frontal was added,. containing a clock dial. The original rose window can still be made out above this.

The tympanum above this door dates from the end of the XIII century. It is carved in three horizontal bands. These show scenes from the infancy of Jesus and the public life of Christ, many of which are based on the Apocryphal gospels. These themes are unique in medieval iconography.

One of the bands shows the wedding at Cana. As this shows the large earthenware jars in the miracle of turning the water into wine, this door also became known as the "Door of the Jars".

Two doors open in the South front:

The Puerta Llana ("Flat Door")

This gets its name from the fact that it has no steps, thereby making it easier for processions to pass through, especially the procession of Corpus Christi with the float on which the Monstrance is mounted. This door used to be called "The Wagon door", as it was through here that the stone was brought in while construction was in progress.

The Ionic style of this door clashes with that of the rest of the Cathedral. It was added in 1800, under the direction of Ignacio Haan, the architect.

La Puerta de los Leones ("The Door of the Lions")

A group of Flemish sculptors arrived in Castille in the middle years of the XV Century. Their leader was Hanequin of Brussels. He came with his brothers, Anton and Egas Cueman, together with Pedro Guas, the father of Juan, who would go on to become the architect of San Juan de los Reyes.

These men introduced the Flemish style to Toledo. Once established in Toledo, they set up a workshop with Toledan artists. This became a centre for the spread of the new forms, and from here came the master artists who were destined to raise the artistic standard of Toledo so high within the country as a whole.

In 1452 the first stone was laid for the **Door of Joy**, in homage to the Assumption. When the railings were added to this door in 1646, it came to be known as the "Door of the Lions" because of the figures holding the shields on the columns.

The group of foreign artists, together with many Toledan stone masons, all under the order of Hanequin, the most important master artist of the Cathedral, worked for eleven years on filling the three sections of the arch around the door with angelic musicians and seraphim. Juan Alemán and Egas Cueman sculpted the statues of the apostles and Marias inside the small atrium.

Only the Virgin above the porch is not the original figure, as it was replaced in the XVIII century with one by Salvatierra.

In the spaces of the two lintels the Transit of the Virgin is shown, according to the text of the Apocryphal gospels, especially that of the Pseudo Joseph of Arimathea.

The Door of the Lions

The meeting of the Apostles in the bedroom, where the Virgin lies in her coffin, is shown on the right. The scene on the left shows the coffin being taken to the Valley of Josaphat. They were attacked by the Jew, Ruben, while on their way, and his dried hands remained stuck to the coffin.

Although Saint Thomas was unable to attend, he watched the Assumption from the Mount of Olives, and the Lady rewarded him by presenting him with her girdle, shown on the small canopy of the Virgin in the division between the doors.

The Aisles

The floor area of the cathedral makes it one of the largest in the Christian world. It is 120 m.s long by 60 m.s wide, and is 33 m. high in the central aisle.

The cathedral is laid out in 5 aisles (with double side aisles). This is a similar floor plan to those at Paris and Bourges, and means that the transept is incorporated into the main body of the church, and is not visible from the outside.

There were a series of attempts at solving the problem of the vaulting of the ambulatory, and the ingenious architect arrived at an original and definitive

Central aisle

solution in Toledo. The vaults were set out in a rectangular pattern, and were triangular instead of trapezoid in shape. This was achieved by using double pillars in the exterior aisles.

The stone framework of this marvel was finished in 1493, during the time of Cardinal Mendoza.

His successors, great prelates and patrons of the arts, were able to use their immense wealth to enrich and decorate the bare stone with chapels, jewels, organs, screens, manuscripts and sculptures. It became one of the most opulent cathedrals in the Christian world.

This process was interrupted by the baroque period, which culminated in the construction of the *Transparente* in 1732.

It is useless to try to avoid cliches in describing Toledo cathedral. In spite of all the robberies and sackings which it has suffered, there can be few places containing so much richness, history and magnificence.

The Mozarab Chapel

The base of the shorter of the two towers used to contain Chapter House. When the Mozarab rite was reestablished under Cardinal Cisneros, he ordered the current Chapter House to be constructed, and dedicated the space in the foot of the tower to the venerable Spanish rite in 1504.

The **spiked grille** in the entrance is one of the best examples of ironwork in the Cathedral. It is unmistakably the work of Juan Francés (1524) and carries the shields of Cisneros and Fonseca.

The **reredos** is composed of Gothic panels of differing origin. The mosaic of the Virgin was ordered by Cardinal Lorenzana, and was made by the most famous Italian artists of the day in the XVIII century. The statue of Christ which crowns the retable was carved from the root of a single bush from the New World, and was donated to the Chapel by a Dominican friar in 1590.

The fine **grille** separating the Choir is a relatively modern work (1920) by the Toledan blacksmith, Don Julio Pascual.

Perhaps the most interesting feature is the **tryptic mural**. This historically interesting work was painted by Borgoña in 1514, and shows the conquest of Orán by Cardinal Cisneros.

Mozarab chapel (detail)

The embarkation of troops with the Cardinal and his Standard bearer at Cartagena is depicted. The landing is shown, and Count Pedro Navarro, who directed miliary operations, also appears. The work is of great historical value, as it was painted only four years after the events shown took place. The details it contains of the attack on the Square, and the equipment, weapons and ships are all of great interest.

The Door of the Lions (interior)

The inside of the Lion Door was transformed in the mid XVI century. Part of Hanequin's work in 1460 was respected, while in perfect harmony with this, the upper part or second wing was successfully added, in the purest Renaissance style.

The doors themselves, with their splendid walnut panels carved by Miguel Copín (son of Diego) and Diego Velasco y Anas, were put into position in 1541.

The inside of the doors are covered with bronze sheets, engraved with amazing skill by Villalpando. The handles of the doors deserve special mention for their refined taste.

Only the niche on the left hand side is occupied, by the elegant mausoleum of the generous canon Don Alonso de Rojas (d. 1577). He was the nephew of Don Francisco, ambassador of the Catholic Kings. The niche on the other side is empty. It was intended for the unfortunate Archbishop Carranza de Miranda, who died in Rome.

The sculpture of the resurrected man in the division between the doors, and the interesting representation of the Tree of Jesse in the tympanum both date from the time of Hanequin (1460).

The symbolic tree of Jesse (the genealogy of the Virgin) does not grow from King David's father's rib, but from his ear.

This is the creation of the Verb, of the Word, which enters through the ears and engenders the idea. As always, the finishing touch is the Virgin and Child.

Above this is a medallion showing the coronation of the Virgin. This is by Gregorio of Burgundy, the son of Felipe. In the side niches there are the figures of David and Solomon, carved by Miguel Copín.

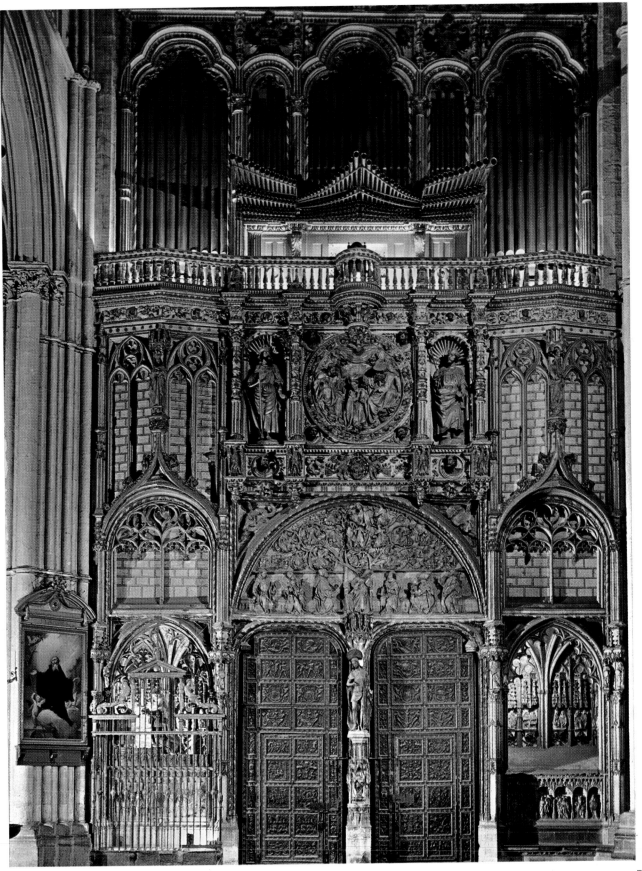

This exceptional facade is crowned by the organ of the Emperor, also known as the Procession organ. This was built by Master organ builder Gonzalo de Cordoba, and was finished by Juan Gaytán, a Toledan, from 1543 - 49.

Although it is now electrified, the old system of supplying air to the organ has been preserved. This consists of two large bellows under each end of a catwalk on a rocker, such that a man had to walk constantly back and forth along the catwalk to pump the air.

The "Transparente"

Several attempts were made at enlarging and illuminating the small room behind the Custody of the High Altar containing the tabernacle where the Holy Vessels are kept.

Cardinal Don Diego of Astorga, who is buried at the foot of the altar, eventually placed Narciso Tomé, a follower of Churriguera, in charge of the works. He worked on the *Transparente* for eleven years, from 1721 to 1732, helped by his sons. He was architect, painter and sculptor while work was under way.

This baroque fantasy of Tomé, who was very much a man of his time, involved the raising of an enormous concave altar screen made of marble and bronze, known as *"the terror of Academics, marvel of the people, always the subject of argument, and always admirable"*.

The centre of the altar holds the small window which lets light through into the sanctuary. Amongst the shining gold leaf are the four archangels Raphael, Gabriel, Michael and Uriel, with their respective symbols around the windows.

The altar itself is made of grey marble. In spite of the vertical, artificial nature of the perspective the scene it of the Last Supper which it depicts is well portrayed. It is crowned by three statues of the Theological Virtues. Tomé worked marble as if it were putty, combining fanciful columns with friezes of angels, and using strangely curved mouldings, embossing and statues, all in one dreamlike work.

A source of light was needed if all this fantasy were to be visible, so with cold audacity he pierced the dome above. He decorated the resulting window with paintings and sculptures to amazing effect.

No other work of art has given rise to so much bitter argument. But no matter what can be said of it, the *transparente* window is a colourful, dynamic and bright spectacle in the stillness and indistinct half-light of the cathedral.

The Chapter House

When the old Chapter House was converted into a Mozarab Chapel, Cardinal Cisneros promised to build a substitute. He made his Head of Works, Pedro Gumiel, and the cathedral architect, Enrique Egas, directors os this project.

The architectural plan is very simple. There is a large rectangular room divided by a thin wall. However, the overall decorative effect is one of exceptional beauty, in what has come to be known as the "Cisneros style". This is the result of the apparently contradictory simultaneous expression of a strong Mudejar influence on a Renaissance style.

There are two archive-cabinets, one on each side of the room. These are in pear tree wood. The one on the left was made by Gregorio Pardo, from 1549-51. He was the son of Felipe de Borgoña, and also worked as his assistant. The one opposite was made to go with the original by Gregorio López Durango in 1780.

The walls were decorated with floral and fruit motifs under the direction of Borgoña in 1511. The flat ceiling decorated with interlocking designs covers the entrance. Blandino Boniface, the last plaster-worker of his kind, moulded the intricate stucco filigrees of the entrance.

The ceiling of the Chapter House is decorated by panels which combine the richness and use of colour of the Renaissance with a Mudejar style of craftsmanship. Richness of colour and design, art and aesthetic appeal are here brought together so harmoniously, and in such splendour, that this is considered to be the most beautiful room in Spain.

Door of the Chapter House

The frescoes are by Juan of Burgundy. Although he had received his artistic education in Italy, he had set up residence in Toledo, where his work gave rise to a school of artists. These frescoes are on the subjects of the Life of the Virgin, the Passion and the Last Judgement. The use of perspective in these frescoes is notable, as is the mix of Florentine, Northern and Toledan influences.

Around the walls in a double frieze are portraits of the Prelates who have occupied the Toledan See, running from Saint Eugene (68 AD) to Pla y Daniel (1968 AD), a total of 1900 years in portraits.

Of the pictures in the upper line, only the portrait of Cardinal Cisneros is taken from life. While some of the others were made using documentary evidence (etchings, statues etc.) the others are clearly imaginary.

In the lower line of portraits, artists contemporary with their subjects have taken their likenesses with varying degrees of artistic success. These pictures are therefore both historically and artistically interesting.

The Chapter House

Rose window

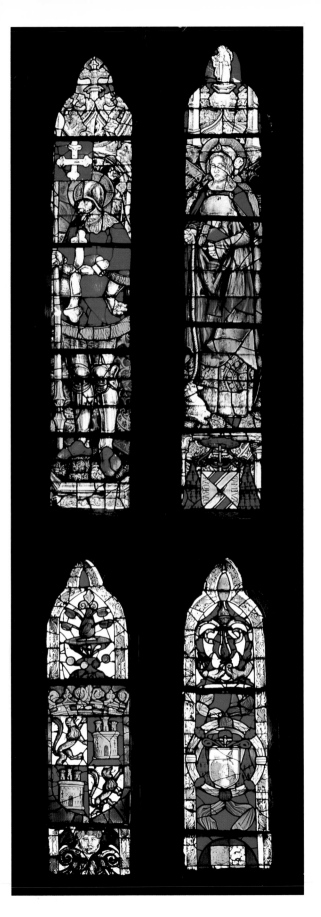

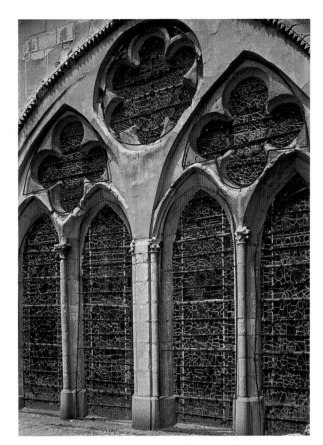

DETAILS OF WINDOWS

63

The Sacristy and auxiliary rooms

Most of the cathedral museums are in the large room of the Sacristy, the Reliquary (an eight - sided room), and the Vestry which leads through to the New Museums.

The vaulted ceiling of the **large Sacristy** is decorated by the Neapolitan artist Luca Giordano (Luca fa presto). It shows the elevation of Saint Idelfonso. The 250 square metres of the ceiling are crowded by brightly coloured people and angels, all within a finely achieved perspective in the painter's unmistakable and effortless style.

The marble altar was placed here in the XVIII Century. El Greco's first masterpiece, the **Spoliation** (1579) hangs above the altar. It was one of the first paintings by the artist in Toledo.

The tunic in this painting is like a red flame, broken by the delicatelypainted hand. The noble, august head of Christ stands out amongst the sinister faces.

On the right of the great painting of the Spoliation are the crown, sword and spurs of Sancho IV, together with the dramatic painting "The Kiss of Judas", one of the few pictures with a religious subject by the great Goya.

On the left - hand side of El Greco's painting, the image of Our Lady of Toledo stands out. It is silver plated, and dates from the XII century. The small boxes are in enamel work from Limoges, and the reliquary in embossed silver containing the arm of Saint Eugene was presented by Saint Luis in the XIII century.

Among the many valuable paintings in this unique exhibition, the collection of the Apostles stands out. The apostles were painted by El Greco several times, although this set is remarkable for its audacity. Here the apostles are shown in flowing, strangely coloured robes. Their expressions are exalted, and El Greco painted some of their faces asymmetrically in his attempt to express the deepest thoughts of those who had been chosen.

The sculpture of Saint Francis of Assisi by Pedro de Mena deserves especial mention, as does the Great Processional Cross in the opposite cabinet. This was presented by Alfonso V of Portugal to Archbishop Don Alonso Carrillo.

A door on the left gives access to the **octagonal room** of the **Reliquary**. This is located behind the Chapel of the Virgin of Sanctuary. The eight sides of this room are walled in red and black marble, decorated with frescoes by Maella (1778).

Many relics in their reliquaries of precious metal are displayed in the niches around the walls. The room is a small museum of embossed, enamelled and shaped metal work.

It contains the "Four Quarters of the Earth", composed of enormous silver spheres made in the XVII century, engraved with maps and the symbols of the continents, and decorated with precious stones.

The small **vestry** is next to the Sacristy. It is full of interesting pictures, and the ceiling was painted by Claudio Coello and Jose Donoso in 1691. It shows the coat of arms of Don Pascual of Aragón, the great patron of the arts who donated his large collection of paintings for exhibition in the Sacristy.

The vestry leads through to the **Room of Ornaments and Robes**. This contains the standard of the Benimerim, which was captured in the Battle of the River Salado, 1340.

The Spoliation (El Greco)

The XIV century English mitre, which belonged to Cardinal Albornoz, stands out in the great collection of rain capes, ecclesiastical robes and mitres of the Toledan Cardinals. There is also a chasuble with the shields of Castile and Aragón, which has been attributed to the infant Archbishop Don Sancho of Aragón, although the heraldic devices would seem to indicate that it was the property of King Don Fernando of Antequera.

The entrance to the "New Museums" is located at the far end of this exhibition. The three floors which they occupy used to be known as "The Treasury". However, a description of these "New Museums" would overstep the limits of this compact guide.

The tears of St. Peter (El Greco)

70   *Saint Francis of Assisi (Pedro de Mena)*

The Chancel

The transformation of the chancel was undertaken by Cardinal Cisneros. The retable used to stand between the column of the Shepherd of Las Navas and that of the Alfaquí, just where the steps end. Behind the retable was the Chapel of the Holy Cross, which had been founded by Sancho IV as a royal pantheon.

On raising the floor for the High Altar, a crypt was created underneath. This contains the mummified body of Saint Ursula, and a group of sculptures on the same subject by Diego Copín de Holanda was also placed there. It is therefore known as the Holy Sepulchre.

To crown the prodigious **High reredos**, a great many wood carvers and their teams were employed under the directorship of Petit - Jean. The fifteen large groups of sculptures, without counting the base, are in larch wood from the forests of Avila. Rodrigo Alemán, Sebastian Almonacid, Bigarny and Copín were among those who worked on this, while two other specialists, Juan Borgoña and Francisco de Ambares, covered the finished work in gold leaf which was then coloured.

The resulting retable is a whole world of fretwork canopies, pinnacles and filigree. It took six years to complete, from 1498 to 1504. The central section begins at the lowest level of the screen above the High Altar. This is a XIV century statue of Saint Mary, covered in silver plate, and came from the earlier retable. Above this is the enormous monstrance, which inspired Enrique de Arfe. As the sanctuary containing the Host is directly behind this, the *Transparente* was constructed 200 years later to illuminate it. The retable continues upwards with representations of Christmas and the Assumption, and is crowned by a gigantic Calvary scene.

The side panels of the retable are decorated with graceful protruding arches. Under these lie the tombs sculpted by Copín de Holanda. On the right are those showing Sancho IV and Maria de Molina, while opposite are those with the figures of Alfonso VII and Doña Berenguela. Nevertheless, the coffins behind these figures actually hold the remains of Sancho IV (d. 1295), the Chapel's founder Alfonso VII (d. 1257), Sancho III (d. 1158) and the child of Alfonso XI, Don Pedro de Aguilar.

Detail of the retable of the High Altar

A first - rate although unknown artist closed off this presbytery with two finesymmetrical fretwork walls at the end of the XIV century.

The one wall still standing is perhaps one of the finest and most poetic works to survive from the Gothic period of Spanish art. This leads on the outside to the procession of the apostles, while inside the frieze shows the Toledan Archbishops. The Kings of Spain were shown on the other wall, but this was unfortunately demolished so that the Renaissance mausoleum of Cardinal Mendoza (d. 1494) could be built. Some of the statues from this wall have been preserved on the pillars inside.

Detail of the retable of the High Altar

The retable of the High Altar

The grille is a worthy finishing touch to this wonderful enclosure, inspired by faith, expressed in art and sealed by history. This fine grille is the most perfect and complete example of Spanish Plateresque style.

The pulpits were founded in bronze and worked by Francisco de Villalpando. He is also responsible for the superb iron grille linking the two. Covered in gold and silver by the method of damascene inlay, the humidity of the atmosphere has harmed the quality of work which it took six years to complete. It was finished in 1548, and is topped by a great crucifix above an imperial shield.

The inside of the choir

The choir is entered through the **grille**, which is by **Master Domingo de Cespedes**. This Toledan ironworker was helped by his son - in - law Hernán Bravo in this great enterprise, the making of which lasted from 1541 to 1548. It is contemporary with the high altar, which is the work of Villalpando.

Master Domingo contracted to make this grille for 6,000 ducats. However, the work lasted for longer than he had thought, the difficulties he encountered were enormous, and so to finish it he not only had to sell all his possessions but also to borrow money.

His anguished pleas for the amount to be paid for the grille to be increased were in vain:

"I have spent all that I earned in my youth on this grille, together with a large sum of maravedies, as I have pawned everything", he wrote to Cardinal Siliceo in 1559. He did receive some help in his poverty, but the great artist died, an example of honesty and integrity, utterly ruined.

The stalls in the **lower choir** are the first work in Spain of Rodrigo Alemán, and took him six years, from 1489 to 1495. The fifty four backs of these stalls are in carefully selected walnut wood. Rodrigo carved these with a historian's eye to show the battles and attacks, fighting and surrenders which had taken place during the memorable time of the conquest of Granada. It is said that during these battles, there were as many heroes as there were captains, and as many brave men as there were soldiers.

These stalls are of immense historical value. The main characters are recognizable, as are the fire arms, military tactics, ways of horse riding and forms of clothing etc. shown. The artist gave free reign to his imagination when carving the designs on the armrests, corners, handrails and decorated brackets of the tip - up seats or "misericords". These contain chimerical animals and burlesque scenes from fables and sayings, in which the artist did not shrink from picturing erotic or even obscene details.

Cardinal Tavera decided to renovate the **upper choir** in 1535. The old one was removed and two first - rate artists were given the job of creating the new one. The left - hand side (facing the altar) was assigned to Felipe de Bigaruy. He was from Burgundy, while the right - hand side is the work of Alonso de Berruguete, a temperamental and emotional artist from Palencia.

Behind the graceful porphyry column, under the series of arches designed by Covarrubias, are the famous walnut panels, the most famous Spanish Renaissance sculpture.

They were carved by Berruguete, who was at the height of his artistic powers. They overflow with fantasy and energy, the tormented and gesticulating figures expressing all the fury of the artist's imagination. Meanwhile Bigaruy, his rival, refined and elegant without abandoning his gothic heritage, calm and classical, died while working on the Archbishop's chair in 1542. The alabaster medallion on this chair is by his brother, Gregorio Pardo, and dates from 1548.

Above the **Archbishop's chair** Berruguete crowned the achievement of the finest and most glorious choir in the world by sculpting the Transfiguration on Mount Tabor, in a single gigantic alabaster block.

The delicate series of arches is complemented by an **alabaster frieze**. This was made by the above - mentioned artists and their assistants, and shows a concise version of the genealogy of Christ, according to the gospels of Saint Luke and Saint Matthew.

Within this unique choir, the **"Prime" (high) Altar** is framed by graceful balusters carved by Rui Díaz del Corral in 1564. The "White Virgin" in marble is French, from the XIV century. Her smiling face and radiant maternal happiness answer the touch of her child.

In the centre is the **great lectern**. The base of this is in the form of a battlemented castle, with figures of the apostles which were brought from Germany in 1425. The great eagle was added in 1646. Its wings are outspread to take the weight of the heavy parchment books used by the choir.

The White Virgin

On either side there is a **bronze lectern**, made by the Vergaras, father and son, in 1570. These lecterns stand on doric columns, which have beautiful golden bronze embossing.

The outside of the Choir

Following the custom in many cathedrals, the perspective in the central aisle is broken by the walls of the **choir**. These walls make it harder to see the shining gold of the retable. The choir was built in the times of Cardinal Tenorio (1376-99). An unfounded tradition holds that the jasper columns on the wall came from the old Arab mosque which previously stood upon this site.

The frieze which runs around the outside of the choir wall is divided into scenes from the books of Genesis and Exodus. The legend of Adam shown here is unique. The frieze is interrupted in the rear choir by the medallion of the Eternal Father. The group of figures of the transfiguration, carved by Berruguete, forms the background to this medallion, and it is flanked by graceful figures representing Guilt and Innocence, by Nicolás de Vergara (1580).

The **three chapels behind the choir**: the central chapel contains a beautiful polychromatic image of the Virgin of the Star (XIV century). The chapel on the right is dedicated to Saint Catalina, while that on the left contains the extraordinary and popular group of the Descent from the Cross, or "Christ lying down". All the figures of which this group is composed can be separated, and they fit together perfectly.

The Cathedral Treasury

Until it was moved by Fonseca to its current location, the three vaults in front of the Treasury formed the **Chapel of the New Kings**. It was here that the Kings of the Trastámara dynasty were buried. The area under the bell tower, where the Treasury is kept today, served as the Sacristy.

The Main Cathedral Treasury. The beautiful facade is by Alonso de Covarrubias, and is crowned by a niche containing the "Quo Vadis" group of figures, with the coat of arms of Archbishop Tavera and workerCanon López de Ayala. As well as being known as "Quo Vadis", this chapel has also been called that of "Saint John" or "The Tower".

The work is Mozarab in style (the stalactites) and is unique in Toledo as it is in wood. It dates from the Trastámara dynasty, and the following display cabinets deserve especial mention:

The first cabinet on the right: this contains a pectoral cross and ring of burnt topazes and diamonds, which belonged to Cardinal Goma. There is also a beautiful cross which was presented by Pope John XXIII, and a chest for the Virgin´s crown.

In the **second display cabinet on the right** a fine three - volume parchment annotated bible stands out. It belonged to Saint Luis, and contains more than 3,000 illustrations.

There is also an engraved silver tray decorated by outstanding work in high relief. This has been attributed to Cellini, although it does bear the stamp: "Matias Melinc. Belgica".

The **Central display cabinet**. This holds the Processional Monstrance for the Consecrated Bread. Standing on an XVIII century pedestal, and supported by four silver plated angels, it is one of the most ostentatious works in precious metals of the Christian world. It was made of silver by the German artist Enrique de Arfe during the early years of the XVI century.

The inner monstrance is made entirely of gold, precious stones and enamel work. It came from the estate of The Catholic Queen, Isabel, and was made by an unknown goldsmith. Tradition has it that the first gold brought from America was used in its making. Its delicate columns enamelled with floral motifs hold the pyx itself, where the consecrated bread is placed.

Enrique de Arfe created this wonderful jewel in the form of a gothic tower during the years 1516 - 1524. It was gold plated at the end of the XVI century.

This monstrance is paraded every year through the streets of Toledo on a special platform, designed to keep it upright over all the slopes and hills of the city.

The small display cabinet on the left holds the imperial crown of the Patron Saint of Toledo. This used to be Queen Isabel´s royal crown, but in 1586 the Toledan jeweller Aloejo de Montoya added the shell, giving it an imperial style. The historical interest of the object itself is heightened by the intrinsic value of the precious stones which it contains. The outstandig emerald in the diamond cross is especially valuable.

The wealth contained in this Treasury is too great to be described in a book of this size.

Up to 64 exhibits are missing. These include the richly decorated mantle of the Virgin of the Sanctuary, which held 80,000 pearls. All of these vanished in 1936.

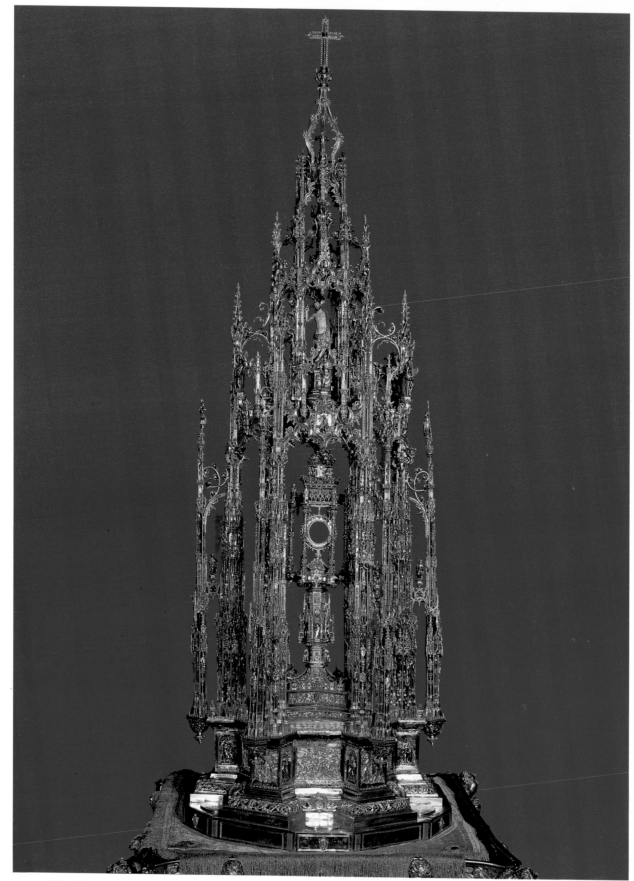

The perimeter walls of the Cathedral are crowded in by nearby buildings, except around the main frontage. The lack of piped water is shown by the activity of the water carriers.

Toledo Town Hall (past)

Toledo Town Hall (present)

Santo Tomé street

The peace and quiet of the Santo Tomé Quarter has been disturbed by the massive influx of souvenir shops, although the buildings themselves remain as they always were.

The Burial of the Count of Orgaz

The burial chapel of Don Gonzalo Ruíz de Toledo, gentleman of Orgaz and Head Notary of Castile, lies at the foot of the church of Santo Tomé. This Toledan nobleman died in 1323 at the end of a pious life, during which he made generous donations to religious institutions.

The legend surrounding his burial had been passed down from generation to generation since his death. According to this legend, those at his funeral were amazed when Saint Augustine and Saint Steven came down from heaven, took up the body and laid it in his tomb. They clearly heard the words: "Such is the reward for those who serve God and his Saints".

The gentleman of Orgaz (who unlike his descendants never had the title of Count) had bequeathed both money and goods in his will to help the priest and poor of the parish of Santo Tomé, to be paid annually by the inhabitants of the town of Orgaz.

Over the years, the people of Orgaz began to avoid making the payments stipulated in the will, and the parish priest took them to court. He won his case, and wanted to commemorate this by placing a painting of the legendary events at the funeral over the tomb of Don Gonzalo Ruíz.

The picture which El Greco painted meets the conditions laid down by the priest, even though it contains contemporary styles of dress and the faces of people alive at the time the picture was painted, making it an anachronism. The resulting work is an exceptional sign of El Greco's arrival at complete artistic maturity.

The contract was signed on Saint Joseph's day, 1586, (March 19th) and the picture was handed over by the artist at Christmas, having taken only nine months to complete.

The painting is divided into upper and lower sections by a line of gentlemen with thoughtful, concentrated expressions, more serene than sad. The levels above and below them are different in both theme and style.

The aged nobility of Saint Augustine, who is supporting the back of the body, contrasts with the youthfulness of Saint Steven, whose hand seems to be holding the legs of the apparently weightless body.

The page in the foreground holding a torch and pointing at the central scene is Jorge Manuel, son of El Greco. The signature on his handkerchief is in Greek, and is dated 1578. This does not coincide with the actual date of the painting, which was finished in 1586. It is actually the year that the boy was born.

The gentleman directly above Saint Steven's head is possibly a self-portrait. He does not seem to be taking part in the burial, and looks out of the painting at those who have come to see it.

The vestments are painted with masterful technique, especially in the details of their embroidery in gold thread. They hang in stately, rigid folds, which contrast with the vibrating light in the delicate white cloth of the surplice, itself a wonderful display of technique.

The physical world ends where the Toledan nobleman are solemnly gathered. Above them, everything changes, and there are clouds, figures and angels painted in an elongated style in arbitrary colours.

Above the group of noblemen there is a blond angel in the centre of a cloudburst. The robes of this angel are being blown upwards by an invisible wind, and the angel is holding a chrysalis. The chrysalis has the form of a new born child, and the angel is trying to push this through the neck of the womb, thereby symbolizing re-birth in God the Father.

The soul abandons its physical remains on the earth, rising up into a perfect triangulation of Christ the Judge, his clothes irradiating luminous white light, and below Him the Virgin on the left and John the Baptist on the right. The two lower figures are intervening on behalf of the arriving soul, and while the Virgin wears flowing blue and carmine robes, John the Baptist has only a sheepskin to cover the nakedness of his disproportionate body.

This painting is a peak of human achievement, and is the artistic heritage of mankind as a whole. It combines technical mastery with a sure hand, inspiration and artistic talent with poetic fantasy and imagination.

The payment lawsuit

The hardships through which El Greco had to pass for two years before he was paid for the "The Burial of the Count of Orgaz" serve as an example of the troubles and difficulties which he suffered every time he was owed money for a painting.

El Greco had received the sum of 46,308 maravedies on starting the painting, as an advance.

Once the painting was finished, the painter and the parish both named their respective valuers. They reached an agreement and valued the work at 1,200 Ducats, or 450,000 maravedies.

The parish of Santo Tomé found this price excessive, as it lacked funds. They therefore asked for the price to be "moderated", and so two new expert valuers were named.

To the immense surprise of the parish priest, these new valuers named a sum 400 Ducats higher than that of the first valuation, setting payment at 1,600 Ducats. As is to be expected, this second valuation was rejected in favour of the first, and the Archbishop's Council found in favour of this payment.

However, El Greco did not accept this judgement, continuing litigation for his demand that the second valuation be paid. He even complained to the Pope. Nevertheless, litigation would have been a long drawn - out process, his creditors would not wait, and the painter was forced to accept the finding of the Archbishop's Council.

The parish priest had only been able to raise 223,882 maravedies, even once he had included his own goods. This sum was paid to El Greco, together with a silver monstrance that could not be used, worth 34,020 maravedies.

The creditors had to wait. Don Andrés Nuñez, the parish priest, said that he would pay them in installments, and he kept his word scrupulously.

Alcántara Bridge

The River Tagus reaches Toledo after winding through fertile agricultural land. At the city it narrows between two granite hills, to follow its course around the rock on which the city is built.

The Al-Qantara bridge lies astride the river just at the point where this narrows. In spite of its Arab name (Al-Qantara means "The bridge") it has Roman origins. This can be seen from the many stone slabs incorporated in its foundations and piers. It was here that the roads linking Toledo to Mérida converged with those going to Cesaraugusta (Zaragoza) via Sigüenza.

The Visigoths maintained and used this bridge. A poem by Venancio Fortunato tells of how Princess Gelesvinta, the daughter of Atanagildo, left on her journey to marry the cruel king of the Franks, Chilperico.

Her parents foresaw her unfortunate destiny, and the wagons loaded with rich goods and the bride's dowry "stopped in the middle of the bridge" for the bitter farewell.

The bridge must have been intact when the Arabs arrived, although it was seriously damaged on several occasions while the central power of Cordoba tried to bring the rebellious city of Toledo under control.

Following a two year siege, Abd -al-Rahman III surrendered Toledo in 932. His first concern was to repair the heavily damaged bridge, which Arab chronicles say had suffered from the Toledan tendency to strive against the Caliph for self - government.

The great flood of 1257, when it rained continuously from August to December, seriously damaged the bridge. The following year Alfonso X "The Wise" had it repaired, reinforcing the giant pier with an enormous cutwater.

One of the original towers still stands. It is on the city side, and was rebuilt in 1484, while Gómez Manrique was chief magistrate. It bears the coat of arms of the Catholic Kings. The completely enclosed fort used to stand on this side of the bridge.

In 1961 the Bab al-Qantara was restored as far as possible. However, the other two walls had been destroyed in 1864 when the road was built.

St. Martin bridge

Alcántara bridge and the Alcázar

The carter crossing Alcántara bridge cracks his whip. In the background, the shield of the Catholic Kings can be seen on the inner bastion of the defenses.

The opposite tower was demolished in 1721, during the reign of Felipe V. An archway was built to replace it, making passage easier for the carts transporting building materials from the nearby tile works.

San Martin Bridge

Toledo used to be supplied with granite for building, coal and other necessities from the mountains of Toledo and Extremadura. A bridge linking the city to the west was therefore needed, and would also have been useful for the passage of cattle.

Experts say that the tower downstream from the bridge, near the walls which here come close to the river, is a remnant of a pontoon bridge which was in existence from Arab times. Known as the **"Baño de la Cava"**, it is associated with the local legend of the love of Don Rodrigo and Florinda.

The old bridge suffered heavy damage from the many battles which took place nearby, and flooding. The floods of 1203 finally destroyed the pontoon bridge, and the construction of a new stone bridge a short way up stream was mooted.

Baño de la Cava and St. John of the Kings

There are no documents showing when work on the new bridge started, and neither is the name of the ingenious architect responsible for the central arch known. However, it is known that it was finished in the early years of the XIV century.

The bridge gets its name from its proximity to the parish dedicated to Saint Martin.

The structure of this bridge was severely damaged during the fratricidal battles between Don Pedro I and his stepbrother Don Enrique. Archbishop Tenorio therefore decided on complete rebuilding, and it was this decision which gave rise to one of the most appealing legends to have sprung from the city.

When the bridge was at an advanced stage of construction, the engineer responsible for the project realized that, once it had been closed and the scaffolding removed, the central arch would not be able to support the weight of the heavy carts bringing in stone for the building of the cathedral. The work of years would be wasted, together with all that the rebuilding had cost. The best that the engineer could hope for himself would be ignominy and a ruined reputation. He told no one, and became more and more depressed with each stone added to the bridge.

Eventually he confided in his wife, but still the work went on, and he could find no solution to the problem.

His wife tried to cheer him up, but one night she crept unseen out of their house, and went to the bridge where after climbing the scaffolding she set light to the thick beams supporting the arch.

Once the supports had burnt through, the unfinished arch of the bridge collapsed. This fire was thought to be due to an unfortunate accident. Work was restarted, and the engineer was able to correct his original calculations. The result is the fine arch of the bridge, spanning 40 metres, 27 metres above the river at the centre.

Legend has tried to give the engineer's resourceful wife her reward for saving her husband's honour and reputation, by saying that the sculpture inserted in the key stone of the bridge is of her face.

However, and in spite of the erosion of the stone which has taken place over the years, the mitred head of the archbishop who ordered the bridge to be restored can still be made out.

St. Martin bridge and Baño de la Cava

St. Martin bridge and St. John of the Kings

Santa Cruz Museum: the main door

Santa Cruz Museum

Renaissance influence was brought to Spain by the Mendoza family, and left its mark on Toledo through the founding of the Santa Cruz hospital by the great Spanish cardinal Don Pedro Gonzalez de Mendoza. He was the son of Don Iñigo, Marques of Santillana.

On his death (2-1-1495) he bequeathed his large fortune to an orphanage. This was dedicated to the Holy Cross (Santa Cruz), and the administrators of his will, Queen Isabel and Cardinal Cisneros, placed the architect **Enrique Egas** in charge of building work. He designed a building in the form of a Greek cross with an Arab style dome in the centre. Four lateral patios are created by this arrangement.

The lintel covered **doorway** shows the scene of Saint Helen and the Holy Cross. This saint was the object of special devotion for the Cardinal. He was born on May 3rd, the same date on which the miracle was commemorated. Covarrubias and Vasco de la Zarza also worked on the building.

Patio of Santa Cruz Museum

Interior view of Santa Cruz Museum

The Veronica (El Greco)

The rooms designed as wards are now given over to a museum holding many of the treasures found in Toledo, too rich and varied to be described here in full.

On the **ground floor** there are many tapestries, amongst which those of the Astrolabe and the one showing the royal coat of arms stand out. There is also the famous figure of Christ, which used to be worshipped in the San Cristo de la Luz mosque, and suits of armour, religious goldsmith work, arquebuses and catapults from the XVI century. These rooms also contain furniture, including cupboards which are richly inlayed. There are two busts of Carlos V, one in silver relief work, the other in marble by Juanelo Turriano. Many of the paintings in the large collection on display are by local painters, especially Comontes, Correa de Vival, Juan de Borgonia and Luis de Carvajal.

The first floor holds paintings by Luis Tristán, Diego de Aguilar, Sánchez - Cotán, and the magnificent standard flown by the flagship in the Battle of Lepanto.

The impressive **"Assumption"** stands out amongst the many paintings by El Greco on display. This is his most daring and lyrical work. He finished it a year before his death (1614). This painting sealed his artistic development, and with its musical rhythms and use of colour is the culmination of all his work.

This painting is the result of El Greco's superhuman effort in the decadence of his old age, a final ecstatic and delirious poem of the spirit.

The Coronation of the Virgin (El Greco)

The Ascension of the Virgin (El Greco)

The Holy Family (El Greco)

"The Hospital de Cardinal Tavera" or "Museum of the Duchess of Lerma"

One of the most interesting museums is to be found housed in the great building of the Hospital founded by Cardinal Tavera. This lies just outside the city walls, opposite the Bisagra Gate.

Designed by the architect Covarrubias, it was the first great Renaissance building to be constructed in Castille. The best artists of the time worked on it during the second half of the XVI Century.

It is divided into two courtyards, separated by a covered passageway, which finally gives onto the beautifully proportioned and well lit church. The Hospital's founder lies here in his own mausoleum, a later work by Berruguete.

Tavera Hospital and partial view

Patio of Tavera Hospital

Tavera Museum Library

A side room holds one of the few apothecary's infirmaries left in Spain. All the tools of the apothecary's trade are on display here, including phials, mortars and scales. The collection of pottery medicine jars deserves especial mention.

The Holy Family (El Greco)

The Hospital was inherited by the descendants of Cardinal Tavera, and eventually came to belong to the Medinaceli family. When the Spanish civil war (1936 - 1939) finished, the Duchess widow of the Duke of Lerma took up residence in one wing of the building, next to the Hospital archives, bringing her art collection with her.

This palace - museum holds many treasures: there is a collection of fine furniture, antique tapestries and carpets, and paintings by El Greco, including "The Holy Family", the "Baptism", one version of "Saint Peter's Tears" and a portrait of the Cardinal taken from his death mask. One picture which is outstanding for its strangeness is the famous "Bearded Woman", signed in 1631 by Ribera.

There is also a portrait of Isabel Clara Eugenia, daughter of Philip II and Isabel de Valois, and Titian's great equestrian portrait of Charles V. This is a copy of the painting in the Prado museum, Madrid.

This combines one of the finest XVI century aristocratic palaces which it is possible to visit in Spain, with one of the country's best collections of art.

Detail from the Holy Family

The Baptism (El Greco)

En magnv natvra
miracvlvm

Magdalena Ventvra ex
oppido Acvmvli apvd
Samnites vvlgo, edo /
Brvzzo regnen. Abrv /
tani annorvm liii et
qvod insolens est cv
annvm xxxvii ageret cœp /
it pvbescere eoqve
barba demissa ac pro /
lixa est vt potivs.

aliqvivs magistri barbati
esse videatvr qvam mv /
lieris qvae tres filios
ante amiserit qvos ex
viro svo felici de amici
qvem adesse vides ha /
bverat.

Iosephvs de Ribera his /
panvs Christi crvce
insignitvs svi tem /
poris alter Apelles
ivssv Ferdinandi II
dvcis III de Alcala /
Neapoli proregis ad
vivvm mire depinxit
xiii kalend. Marti.
anno M.D.C.XXXI.

The Cathedral with the bell tower of the old clock (demolished in 1888) stands out against a background of the flat walls of the convents, and the unique geometrical forms of the roofs on the hillside. The Alcázar can be seen in the rear of the picture, as it was before it suffered the massive fire which completely destroyed it a year later.

The Alcázar and its museums

Dominating the houses crowded on the Cervantine hill, *"glory of Spain and light of its cities"*, stands the imposing bulk of the Alcázar (royal palace).

This site was doubtless used by the Romans as a praetorium (military base). The line followed by the Roman wall of "Toletum" started here, to go down to the Arco de la Sangre (the "Arch of Blood" in Zocodover). Remains can still be seen in the Calle de las Armas, on the way down to the Paseo del Miradero.

Nothing remains of Visigoth times here. Nevertheless, the door in the south west corner dates from the period of Arab domination, from the time of Abd - al-Rahman (835).

Alfonso VI rebuilt the Alcázar on the reconquest of the city. Tradition has it that the first governor was El Cid, who stationed his Castilian and Aragonese troops here.

The Toledan King Alfonso X "The Wise" caused the east wall to be built in the XIII century. The battlements of this wall and its turrets can still be seen.

In one of the underground rooms of the Alcázar, the bedroom of Doña Blanca, unfortunate wife of Don Pedro I "The Cruel" has been reproduced. This is to commemorate the days which she spent imprisoned here.

It was Carlos V who adapted and converted the building into a royal palace. For this he employed the finest architects of his day, including Covarrubias and Juan de Herrera.

Partial view and the Alcázar

Once the royal court had moved definitively to Madrid, the Alcázar was occasionally still used for royal visits. The first of the major fires which it has suffered occurred during the Wars of Succession in 1710.

A hundred years later, in 1810, Napoleon's troops set fire to the building when they left the city. It was taken over for use as an Infantry Academy in 1846.

It was the scene of heroic resistance during the Spanish Civil War (1936) when it was besieged. Once again, it suffered grave damage.

It was rebuilt once again, now containing a museum of the siege, and the Museum of Knives and Swords in a large room. The exhibition shows how this science has developed from stone knives to the famous blades of Toledo steel. Another exhibition holds a collection of fire - arms, from the earliest days of gunpowder down to modern automatic weapons. Yet another museum holds trophies, souvenirs and uniforms from the times when Spanish troops were in Africa. The Alcázar also houses the Romero Ortiz collection of historic objects and medals.

The Alcázar before the fire

St. Elizabeth Street

The old beams have given way beneath the weight of time, and have been propped up by wooden supports. What was once an aristocratic mansion has now become a public courtyard.

GENERAL INDEX

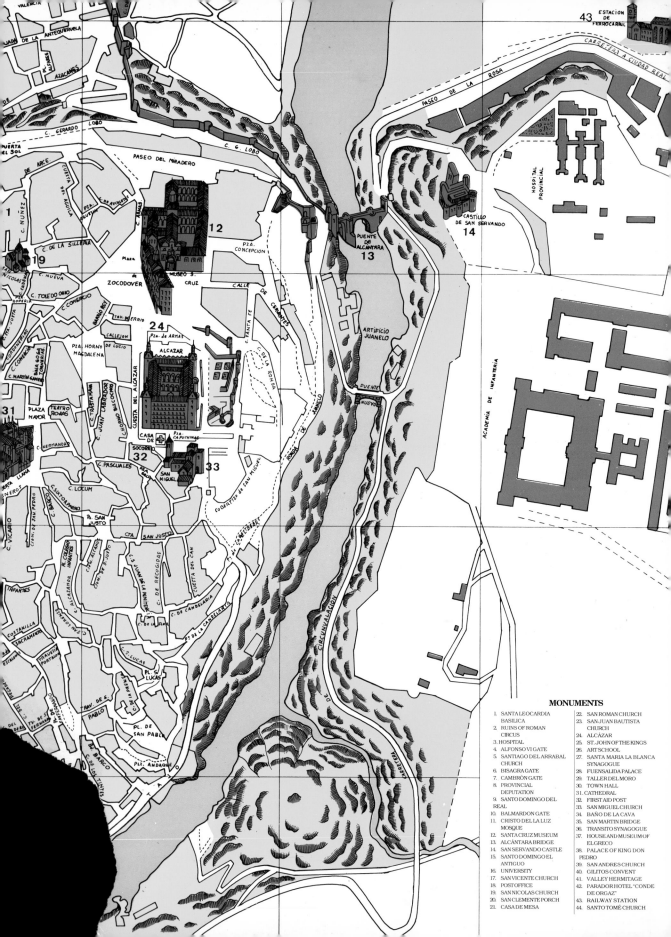

MONUMENTS

1. SANTA LEOCARDIA BASILICA
2. RUINS OF ROMAN CIRCUS
3. HOSPITAL
4. ALFONSO VI GATE
5. SANTIAGO DEL ARRABAL CHURCH
6. BISAGRA GATE
7. CAMBRÓN GATE
8. PROVINCIAL DEPUTATION
9. SANTO DOMINGO DEL REAL
10. BALMARDON GATE
11. CRISTO DEL LA LUZ MOSQUE
12. SANTA CRUZ MUSEUM
13. ALCÁNTARA BRIDGE
14. SAN SERVANDO CASTLE
15. SANTO DOMINGO EL ANTIGUO
16. UNIVERSITY
17. SAN VICENTE CHURCH
18. POST OFFICE
19. SAN NICOLAS CHURCH
20. SAN CLEMENTE PORCH
21. CASA DE MESA
22. SAN ROMAN CHURCH
23. SAN JUAN BAUTISTA CHURCH
24. ALCÁZAR
25. ST. JOHN OF THE KINGS
26. ART SCHOOL
27. SANTA MARIA LA BLANCA SYNAGOGUE
28. FUENSALIDA PALACE
29. TALLER DEL MORO
30. TOWN HALL
31. CATHEDRAL
32. FIRST AID POST
33. SAN MIGUEL CHURCH
34. BAÑO DE LA CAVA
35. SAN MARTIN BRIDGE
36. TRANSITO SYNAGOGUE
37. HOUSE AND MUSEUM OF EL GRECO
38. PALACE OF KING DON PEDRO
39. SAN ANDRES CHURCH
40. GILITOS CONVENT
41. VALLEY HERMITAGE
42. PARADOR HOTEL "CONDE DE ORGAZ"
43. RAILWAY STATION
44. SANTO TOMÉ CHURCH